This is Zion

An interpretation of a colorful
landscape in picture and story.

By

Allen Hagood
Former Park Naturalist

Published by the
Zion Natural History Association

in cooperation with the
National Park Service

U. S. Department of the Interior

Second Edition

Printed in the United States of America by
DESERET PRESS
Salt Lake City, Utah
1969
Reprinted 1980
ISBN No. 0-915630-06-0

*Front Cover—Temples and Towers of
the Virgin from Zion Visitor Center.*

*Left—Taylor Creek road and Pine
Valley Mountains from Beatty Point.*

*Slickrock and clouds, flowing forms and
changing colors, a summer afternoon at Zion.*

Great White Throne.

Introduction

This book was to have been an account of Zion's geological history. However, we realized that a pictorial approach would appeal to visitors who seek a general appreciation of the scenery. In following a theme of beauty in stone, much information on the origin of Zion landscapes has been included.

The enthusiasm and enduring patience of numerous field companions improved the quality of photographs taken in the back country. All color pictures and the black and white pictures not credited were taken by the author with a 4 x 5 camera.

I am grateful for permission to reprint excerpts from the following books: *Beyond the Hundredth Meridian*, by Wallace Stegner (Houghton Mifflin Company); *The Physics of Blown Sand and Desert Dunes*, by R. A. Bagnold (Methuen and Company); and *Utah Historical Quarterly* (Utah State Historical Society).

The Zion Natural History Association sponsored the illustration and publication of this book. The Association is a non-profit organization dedicated to interpreting the aesthetic and environmental values of Zion National Park. Information on the publications and activities of the Association may be obtained by writing to the Executive Secretary, Zion Natural History Association, Zion National Park, Springdale, Utah 84767.

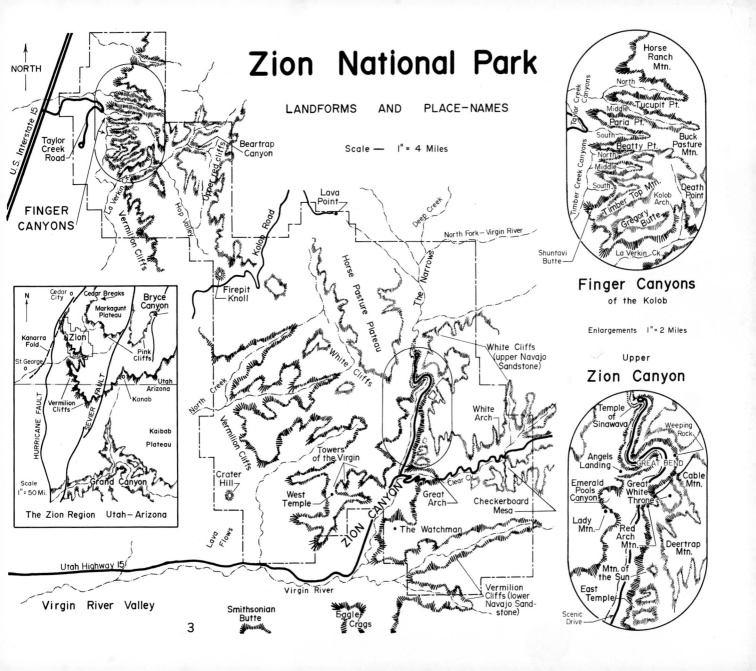

Zion National Park

LANDFORMS AND PLACE-NAMES

Scale — 1" = 4 Miles

Finger Canyons
of the Kolob

Enlargements 1" = 2 Miles

Upper
Zion Canyon

3

References

1. Bagnold, R. A., 1954, *The Physics of Blown Sand and Desert Dunes:* Methuen and Company, Ltd., London, page xxi.

2. Brooks, Juanita, 1961, *Utah's Dixie, the Cotton Mission—The Face of the Land:* Utah Historical Quarterly, vol. 29, no. 3, page 196.

3. Dutton, Clarence E., 1882, *Tertiary History of the Grand Canyon District:* U. S. Geological Survey Monograph No. 2, U. S. Government Printing Office, Washington, D. C., pages 36-37 and 57-60.

4. Gregory, H. E., 1950, *Geology and Geography of the Zion Park Region, Utah and Arizona:* U. S. Geological Survey Professional Paper No. 220.

5. Kurie, Andrew E., 1966, *Recurrent Structural Disturbance of Colorado Plateau Margin Near Zion National Park, Utah:* Geological Society of American Bulletin, vol. 77, no. 8, pages 867 - 872.

6. Opdyke, George H., 1932, *Art and Nature Appreciation:* Macmillan Company. Reprinted 1959 by National Council Books, Inc., Philadelphia.

7. Palmer, William R., 1933, *Pahute Indian Homelands:* Utah Historical Quarterly, vol. 6, no. 3, page 99.

8. Powell, John W., 1895, *Canyons of the Colorado:* Flood and Vincent. Reprinted 1961 by Dover Publications, page 297.

9. Stegner, Wallace, 1953, *Beyond the Hundredth Meridian:* Houghton Mifflin Company, Boston, pages 122-123.

10. Woodbury, Angus M., 1950, *A History of Southern Utah and Its National Parks:* Privately published, page 199. (Formerly in Utah Historical Quarterly).

Left—Platforms and cliffs of Zion. Eroded layers of rock give horizontality to the land.

Contents

Through long ages, the earth's crust in this region slowly sank. The rocks of Zion accumulated in layers as sediment washed onto the lowlands. At one time, sand dunes smothered the river plains, and the resulting desert layer, now turned to stone, exhibits striking patterns.

Widespread sinking of the earth's crust was replaced by upheaval. This change resulted first in folding of the layered rocks and later in eruption of volcanoes. Finally, the rocks were uplifted in plateaus, and the stone was broken by many fractures which promote erosion.

Gravity and running water sculpture the tablelands into wide canyons and narrow gorges. On a lesser scale, the rocks are etched into fascinating forms, and their surfaces are stained with vivid colors. Much beauty in stone results from the erosional destruction of Zion.

Zion's history follows the world-wide and age-old cycle of deposition, uplift, erosion and redeposition. The Virgin River is returning the ancient sediment of Zion's rocks to its original condition—in layers near sea level.

Part One

The Beauty of Zion

Many individuals and cultures have contributed to our interpretation of Zion's beauty.

A Long Road to Understanding—Zion's first known inhabitants, the Basketmakers, left little record of their attitudes toward the land.

Later Indians, the Paiutes, had wary feelings about these canyons. Paiutes were animists; they believed that vitality pervades all matter and that inanimate things such as rocks had souls and could move of their own volition. The Towers of the Virgin, a site of frequent rockfalls, was known to them as Rock-Rovers-Land (Ref. 8). Mischievous spirits were said to have kindled fires on one of the inaccessible spires. That legend could have some basis, for lightning-set blazes occur almost every summer on the forested tabletops. Despite the fears of some Paiutes, one clan called the loogune-intz, or People-who-live-in-a-sack, lived at the mouth of Zion Canyon and grew corn and squash up the valley for a considerable distance (Ref. 7).

Paiutes told colorful legends about the creation of this land. These were stories of

Mountain of the Sun and Zion Canyon from Deertrap Mountain, early morning.

East Temple, late afternoon. Erosion breaks the jointed walls into columns.

6

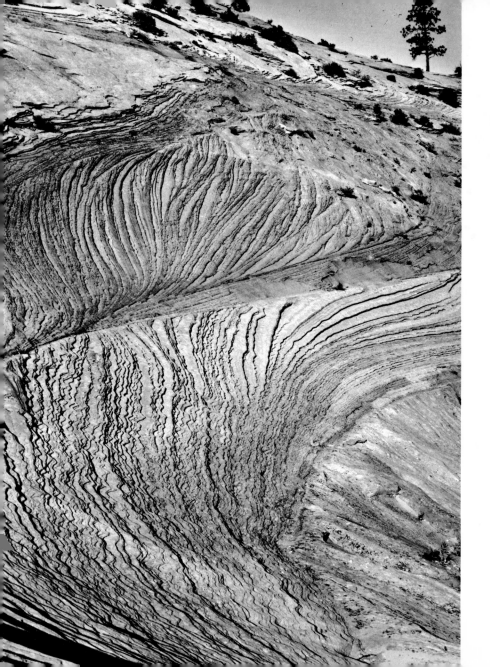

a people vulnerable to the forces of nature. The Indians were resigned to their role as creatures of a harsh environment. They belonged to Zion in fact, whereas we only imagine it belongs to us. A strange new philosophy of land use which originated across the sea and endures to present was on the way.

Onto the scene came European man who displaced the Indians and aggressively reaped the sparse resources of the land. Pioneer journals contain few descriptions of the landscapes that we now consider beautiful. Identification of beauty stopped where the productive riverlands ended and the rocky slopes began. In the Nineteenth Century, arid natural scenes were seldom romanticized by anyone. Many Americans felt that fertile pastures and fields—not barren deserts and plateaus—should be idealized. With poetic frustration, Parley Pratt, an explorer of 1849, wrote of one southern Utah landscape: "... *no signs of water or fertility . . . a wide expanse of chaotic matter . . . consisting of huge hills, sandy deserts, cheerless grassless plains, perpendicular rocks, loose barren clay, dissolving beds of sandstone . . . lying in inconceivable confusion, in short, a country in ruins dissolved by the peltings of the storms of the ages and turned inside out, upside down, by terrible convulsions in some former age . . ."* (Ref. 2).

Crossbedded sandstone and lone pine tree near East Entrance of Zion National Park.

Drifting pink dunes near Zion recreate in small scale the sand seas of Navajo times.

A few explorers were not seeking sites for immediate settlement. In 1872, U. S. Government scientists and surveyors of the Powell expeditions visited Zion. In their official publications, Zion first received attention as a place of scenic grandeur. Powell and his colleagues gave the Plateau Province, "... *a rudimentary aesthetics, used it as a starting point for a curious and provocative inquiry into the sublime and beautiful, and strengthened the affinity that Turner and Ruskin had established between geology and art,*" (Ref. 9).

Clarence Dutton, a Powell geologist, wrote eloquently of Zion: "... *As we rode along, there sailed slowly and majestically into view, a wonderful object ... In coming time it will, I believe, take rank with a very small number of spectacles each of which will, in its own way, be regarded as the most exquisite of its kind which the world discloses. The scene before us was the Temples and Towers of the Virgin ... There is an eloquence to their forms which stirs the imagination with a singular power, and kindles in the mind of the dullest observer a glowing response ... Directly in front of us a complex group of white towers, springing from a central pile, mounts upwards to the clouds. Out of their midst, and high over all, rises a dome-like mass, which dominates the entire landscape ...*

Sand seas of the Empty Quarter, Saudi Arabia. Dunes about 500 feet high. The crossbedded layers of Navajo Sandstone at Zion may have formed under similar conditions. Arabian American Oil Company photo by T. F. Walters, courtesy of Donald Holm.

Pools and potholes in Navajo Sandstone.

ROCK FORMATIONS
of Zion National Park

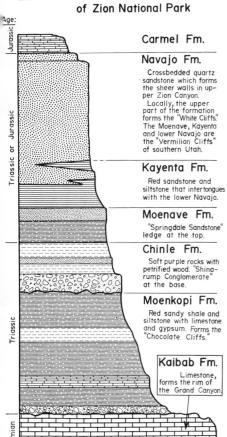

"Pink Cliffs formation" is much higher.

Age:

Jurassic

Triassic or Jurassic

Triassic

Permian

Carmel Fm.

Navajo Fm.
Crossbedded quartz sandstone which forms the sheer walls in upper Zion Canyon.
Locally, the upper part of the formation forms the "White Cliffs." The Moenave, Kayenta and lower Navajo are the "Vermilion Cliffs" of southern Utah.

Kayenta Fm.
Red sandstone and siltstone that intertongues with the lower Navajo.

Moenave Fm.
"Springdale Sandstone" ledge at the top.

Chinle Fm.
Soft purple rocks with petrified wood. "Shinarump Conglomerate" at the base.

Moenkopi Fm.
Red sandy shale and siltstone with limestone and gypsum. Forms the "Chocolate Cliffs."

Kaibab Fm.
Limestone, forms the rim of the Grand Canyon.

Enormous tilted prows of the Finger Canyon buttes are eroded in layered rocks on the side of Kanarra Fold.

Bear Trap Canyon, a shady green oasis typical of the Kolob.

Nothing can exceed the wonderous beauty of Little Zion Valley, which separates the two temples and their respective groups of towers . . . In its proportions it is about equal to Yosemite, but in the nobility and beauty of the sculptures there is no comparison. It is Hyperion to a satyr. No wonder the fierce Mormon zealot, who named it, was reminded of the Great Zion, on which his fervid thoughts were bent—'of houses not built with hands, eternal in the heavens,' '' (Ref. 3).

In the decades after Dutton's visit, Zion was publicized by the photographs of Jack Hillers, the paintings of Frederick Dellenbaugh, and the writings and lectures of Frederick Vining Fisher. Stephen T. Mather, the first director of the National Park Service, was impressed by Zion's little known beauty, and he felt it was truly of national significance. Congress agreed, and Zion became a national park.

Many visitors come to the parks to draw inspiration from the scenery. To say the national parks have become popular is understatement. As in the case of overloved children, we risk spoiling them.

Man and Nature at Zion—Man is a major force in shaping the course of nature on earth. But he is a force without definite direction to ensure his continued well being.

That man is in conflict with his environment is seen in his dual desire to **use** and to **preserve** the landscapes in national parks. It is not realistic to think that the parks are separate from the rest of the world. People who come here to "get away from it all," may be disturbed to find that "it all" is insidiously at work at Zion.

Man has gradually divided Zion into two parts. One part contains the visitors and their facilities, and the other

Fossil dinosaur tracks on slabs of Kayenta shale, North Creek. In rocks are records of ancient environments.

Waterfall after thundershower, Temple of Sinawava.
U. S. Geological Survey photo by J. C. Anderson.

15

part is the scenery and natural beauty. Fortunately for the Park Service, people on vacation in "reasonable" numbers seem to enjoy each other. There is a limit to tolerance, however, when people trying to escape crowds in the cities realize they are elbow to elbow in the country. A common reaction to this type of pressure is, "Why doesn't the Park Service spread the facilities beyond this narrow canyon?"

National parks, like all land areas, are finite. Only so much area can be developed before facilities begin to compete with nature's serenity. For example, from the new Taylor Creek road in the Kolob area of the park, visitors look into the Finger Canyons. They are thrilled to see the spectacular gorges, and they are interested in the wilderness lying before them. Yet the road as seen from the canyons is an intrusion on the landscape, and the wilderness seems less than wild, tamed perhaps. Here is an unintentional psychology in reverse, akin to a situation in zoos where caged wild animals might wonder if the world outside is on exhibit. In the positioning of the new road, perspective may have gone awry.

Meanwhile, in Zion Canyon, the density of modern human culture increases, and there is mounting pressure to pave more scenery with campgrounds and parking lots. We are party to a strange paradox.

A wilderness trail through the Kolob.
Summer afternoon in LaVerkin Creek Canyon.

The patterns of ancient desert cross-bedding. Motion frozen in stone.

Wilderness is as much concept as condition. Without imagination, the idea of nature in the wild would have little meaning. To some of us, wilderness is ten feet from the pavement; to others, it is complete solitude miles from roads. Wilderness to suit almost everyone's taste lies relatively close to Zion Canyon. Yet the epitome of wilderness is in the Kolob far to the northwest. Few places in the world compare to the Kolob for majesty of land forms and impact of coloration. It is the hidden showcase of Zion, a vivid land still little troubled by tourism.

The salmon-pink stone and rich green vegetation of the Kolob remind some people of disarrayed color in a shattered watermelon. Forests of the mesa tops break sharply at overhanging precipices (photo, page 28). On north-facing walls where plants thrive and decay, black carbon tapestries descend hundreds of feet into eternal shadow.

The most delicate hues in Zion are mixtures of colored reflections in shade. This quality of light is seen throughout the park, but in the deep canyons of the Kolob, it is most inspiring. In the Finger Canyons, where sandstone walls glow pink from top to bottom, vibrant recitals are played on color organs. These are not audible melodies, but visual chords which work delightful confusion on the senses. People who

Wall at head of Emerald Pools Canyon. Rockfall on a springline, the face of erosion.

Winter sunrise on West Temple and Towers of the Virgin from Zion Visitor Center.

come looking for effect may find they are listening to it instead. Suddenly, we sense a vitality in all matter around us as if there were life even in air and rock. With such synesthetic sensations, we begin to wonder if we, like the Paiutes, have become animists.

Indians saw the Creation wonderously in terms of their limited world. Today's world is different. We have an elaborate technology that grasps for possibly unreachable secrets of the Universe. Never have there been such horizons for inspiration and discovery. Where, then, is our sense of wonder? Perhaps trapped beneath the pavement of the freeways or enmeshed in the woven landscape of suburbia.

Deep in the Finger Canyons there is intoxicating immediacy, a beauty "here and now" that vaporizes our worries of the world outside. Vivid walls catch sunlight and splash the warm reflections into shadows far below. The understory glows with incredible richness, a red to purple luminescence that suffuses in all directions, seemingly as a chromatic gas that is visible unto itself. There is quivering motion as dust shimmers in canyon currents. Even on quiet days, color is seen as if cast through a tremulous veil. Here the material qualities of air remind us that we live on

Eagle Crags, dynamic sky. Zion lies in a corrosive sea of air and moisture.

Autumn along a stream in the Kolob.

Following Page—Crossbedded sandstone.

21

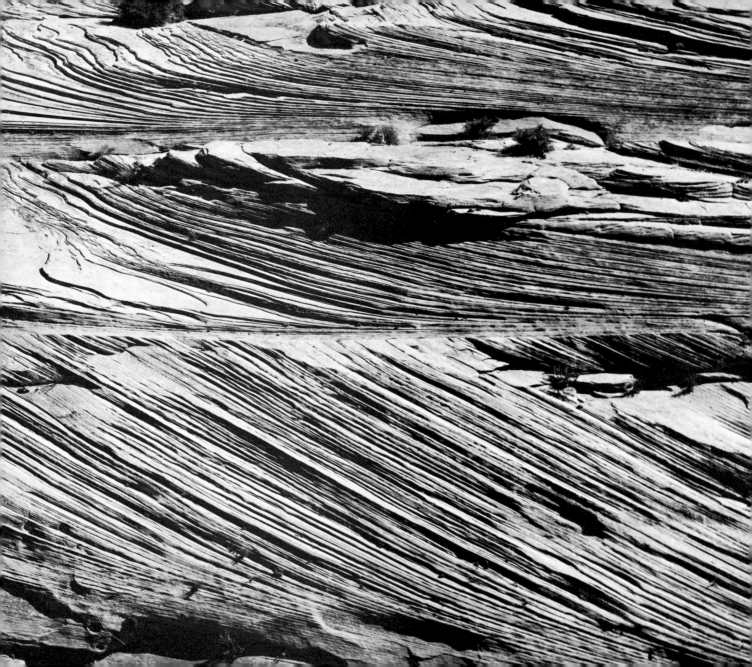

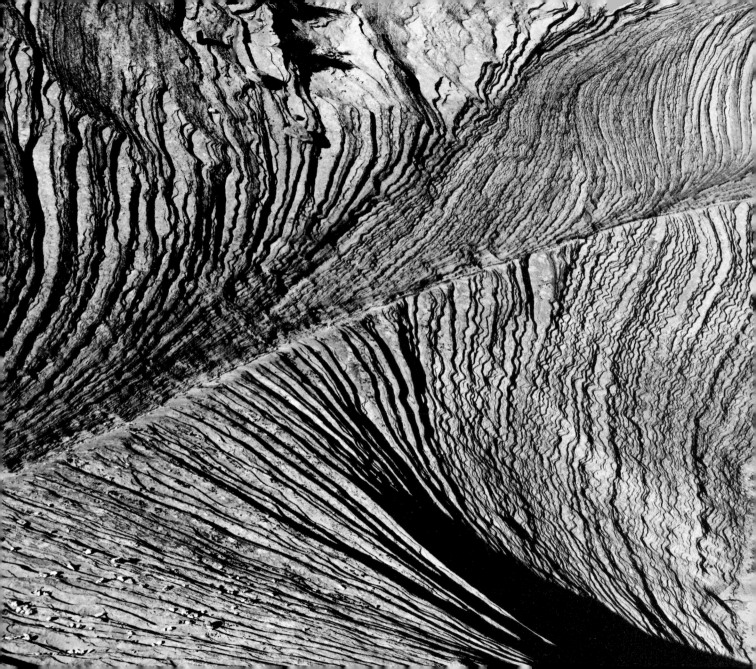

the bottom of an atmospheric ocean—the same air shared with all the cities of the world. A jet thunders overhead and trails a white "sky worm". At once, we awaken to reality—the spreading world of industrial man.

A View from Space—Perspective is our mental ability to move beyond the present time and place to other viewpoints. Perspective clarifies, averts disasters, offers solutions. Photos from manned Apollo flights provide some startling views.

In perspective from space, the overall shape of the earth's crust seems to conform to Universal law. We may have thought that Zion was grandly unique, but the unearthly view suggests its origins do not differ significantly from other lands.

In looking back at Earth, we become visually aware that matter in space can gather in spheres. Gravity keeps heavenly bodies spherical, and it resists the tendencies in nature—such as mountain building forces in the earth's crust—to distort the curvature. On an unusual globe such as Earth where water is active on the surface, gravity has a mighty ally in its mania to maintain spherosity. From air laden with water vapor comes rain, and water on land in gravity's clutch is erosion.

Preceding Page—Sandstone symphonies, the visual music of crossbedding.

Angels Landing and "Walters Wiggles" trail from the south wall of Refrigerator Canyon.

West Temple after late spring storm.

24

Thus, the earth's crust has been upheaved and worn down time and again. In the cycles of uplifting and downtearing, mud and sand have been washed into low places, and these sediments have been spread in layers and become new rock. Zion is made of many such layers.

Plants and animals, the species of the past, were no less dependent upon their particular habitats than are living things at present. Remains of life in rock, known as "fossils," are found in the sedimentary layers deposited through time. A rock layer may have formed in an environment much different than the layers above or below. Thus, the general types of fossil plants and animals can change abruptly from layer to layer.

Mountains, rivers, deserts, swamps, and the sea; evidence of all these habitats and their living things are found in rocks of the Zion region. By studying rocks and fossils, we see in the many environments through time an incredible panorama of life.

We marvel at the adjustments life must have made to changing conditions. Most species could not adapt. For example, in the diverse group, dinosaurs, many were long-lived, but finally none survived. Will man be as successful? Can he even match the dinosaurs for longevity of stay on this tortured planet? In the book of time in which pages

Joints and waterfall above Upper Emerald Pool. Erosion follows the grain of the land.

The Watchman, a study in pyramids. In horizontal and vertical lines is the architectural unity of Zion.

are made of rock, we see ourselves in different perspective. And mankind envisioned from space is even more distressing.

Until this decade, we looked out to the stars. Now we look in from the Universe, and we see the fair green hills of Earth in perplexing new light. Within the thin skim of clouds is most of the air we breathe. That skin of life-giving gas is all that matters to you and me. At last check, the black coatings on Zion's walls were still desert varnish, not industrial tarnish. Will it always be?

Early man was but part of the natural environment. Then our species changed, and man's manipulation was refined to unbelievable subtlety, unthinking grossness. Man swept the globe, reducing the miraculous diversity of Earth to a single monotonous environment—his own. Why? What prompts his impatience with nature? Why is his individual success rooted in his ability to manipulate? Is he simply a superior animal seeking creature comforts? Or is civilized man so new a being that he is not free from all distrust and fear of nature?

Whatever the underlying reason, maybe part of our sense of wonder becomes fuel to man's wanton industrialization of Earth. Curiosity moves us to exciting discovery. We feel comfortable—or fulfilled—when we find explanations for natural phenomena. But beyond inspiration and satisfaction

Middle Canyon of Taylor Creek from Tucupit Point. Pink cliffs and hanging forests.

North Canyon of Timber Creek from Beatty Point. Bare rock and forested niches.

29

with mere explanation, we are urged to conquer and to improve on nature.

Can man, being part of nature, hope to conquer it? That is the point. Man has nothing to gain and much to lose when he works against himself.

The idea that man can improve on nature is valid relative only to man. The benefits of a natural process made more efficient by man go directly to man; but deleterious effects may be thoughtlessly turned back to nature. Nature is often treated as a sewer that will absorb refuse indefinitely.

In forgetting that he depends fully on nature, man often attaches significance to information in useful fragments and ignores the whole. When minor effects of Universal law are identified, technicians find ingenious ways to use the little secrets of nature to further human progress. Sometimes "progress" alone dictates the decisions, and no one asks if the "advance" is entirely beneficial. Secrets of nature overused or put in wrong combination disrupt the delicate natural systems which were ages in the making. From these systems, we draw materials and energy for our lives. From them, too, comes inspiration for our art.

Color-washed wall and red earth in Double Arch alcove, Middle Canyon of Taylor Creek.

Near Right—Yellow foliage and pink and purple streaks on ledge, Kolob wilderness.

Far Right—Blossoming yucca and carmine streaks on sandstone wall, White Cliffs.

Industrial man has set himself artificially apart from nature. He does not take alarm at deterioration of the environment because many of the warning signs are seen as progress. He thinks in parts while serving his technology, and he is not accustomed to looking at the whole environment.

Man of the land, in spirit at least, has better access to facts of human well being. He reaps only the dividends of nature's systems, knowing better than to draw on the capital. He tries to be a global citizen, sensing the indivisibility of all the garden plots on Earth. There are no independent actions by man in nature. Move a grain of sand and you change the stars.

Our Search for Beauty—Zion is part of the cosmos. In these landscapes is evidence of the physical laws which have ruled on Earth for billions of years. At first, it is hard to see this order in the confusion of nature.

Walls collapse and stone pillars topple when water erodes the softer rock beneath. Chaos seems to reign at Zion until we tune our senses to nature's broader schemes. He who seeks this order in nature becomes personally conscious of beauty. Zion is for inspired men who set their imaginations free to find loveliness in common things closeby.

Should general scenery—the broad vistas—be the sole object of a visit to a

White on black. A thin layer of limestone weathers onto a carbon-stained wall.

Autumn foliage and mineral stain, rock bench, wilderness canyon in the Kolob.

32

national park? Some people think so. They despair because their cameras don't have wide-angle lenses to take in all the canyon walls which rise near at hand. However, in gathering only the huge, general impressions, they may ignore worthwhile details. In learning how the details fit together as an orderly whole, we build avenues of quiet confidence that lead to discovery of beauty.

The search for beauty may begin by studying small patterns: the textures of natural surfaces, the sweep of curving lines, the mosaics of light and shadow. And foreseeing the interplay of light in nature is fulfilling too; a scene flatly illuminated may lack artistic character, whereas the same view when the sun is at a different angle may be an exquisite composition.

Appreciation of nature is not instinctive to most of us. A lady told me as she first began noticing forests that they were very unorderly places. On later trips to the woods, she began picking out certain patterns that pleased her. Without camera or paintbrush, she began realizing what artists know: that art is inspired by nature, but the artist must select from nature's hodgepodge that which touches the sensitivity of his human audience. Willis Lee, a Yale lecturer, noticed the confusion in nature at Zion when he said, *"In a sense, Zion resembles a museum where so many unusual objects are crowded together that the mind is bewildered and the eye tires."* Nature is truly a hodgepodge until we edit it for our use or enjoyment.

Checkerboard Mesa, horizontal crossbedding and vertical cracks formed by weathering.

Beauty exists only in the individual mind. People bring their own aesthetic values when they come to Zion, but they may depart having become aware of beauty in terms they had never thought of before. We hope through direction of personal discovery that your expectations of Zion are realized or exceeded.

Beauty in Stone—The rest of this book covers only one of nature's systems of order. The story is about rock and how beauty may be seen within it. Soon it will become apparent that rock is neither dull nor immovable. In fact, the ever-present hint of change in stone is the key to its beauty.

To find beauty at Zion, you could begin by exploring patterns of color on rock walls deep in canyons (photo, page 67). Where water trickles onto cliffs, it leaves its residues in streaks. Nature drapes her springlines with bright curtains, and she decks her stony benches with vivid tapestries (photos, pages 31 and 33).

At the top of canyon walls, vermilion muds streak down sheer walls, reminding us of blood. Erosion saps the strength of stone and forebodes the destruction of landscapes. From the cliffs of Zion flow the colorful cements that bind grains of sand and give solidity to rock. **Much beauty in stone issues from the very forces that tear down the land.**

Thus, it seems that beauty results from disorder at Zion. This idea would be a contradiction to what has been written earlier

Spherical concretions, marble-size. Iron-rich balls weathered from Navajo Sandstone.

35

were it not for our learning in the pages to follow that erosion is part of a grand order not readily visible.

Part Two . . .

The Geological Story

Throughout the history of Earth, there has been ceaseless erosion of uplifted lands and downward movement of the resulting sediment into low places. Our story tells of the birth, uplift, deterioration and removal of the stone which composes Zion. These rocks, laid down as sand and mud, were disrupted by earth movements and were uplifted in plateaus. As uplift continues, the rocks are eroded, and their fragments are carried seaward in rivers. Thus, Zion is seen as part of an erosional cycle which is repeated time and again over the Earth.

The Layered Rocks of Zion...

There would be no Zion without the towering cliffs eroded in Navajo Sandstone. In upper Zion Canyon, this two-thousand-foot-thick layer dominates the scene. It obscures the underlying rocks and the stories they tell. A full understanding of the landscape is lost to those who do not take time to see beyond the main canyon.

Timber Top Mountain and Shuntavi Butte, sunset.
A crimson prow sinking in evening shadows.

36

The best way to see the rocks and to understand their creation is to approach the park from the southwest. Along the Virgin River valley, sheer canyon walls are not prominent. We see instead the broad, terrace-like mesas in which brick-red tiers of rock mount in steps to the blue horizon. The road parallels the Chocolate and Vermilion Cliffs, and we come ever closer to the scenic threshold at the mouth of Zion Canyon (photo, page 59).

A Land of Platforms and Cliffs—Zion's foundation stones are conspicuously tabular, and the rock stands out in flat-lying layers. This large-scale framework is of first importance to the story.

Gravity and running water expose the horizontal grain of the land and etch it into platforms and cliffs. Some of the layers are hard, like sandstone and limestone; others, like shale and siltstone, are soft. Running water removes the soft layers more rapidly and leaves the edges of hard layers protruding in relief. In broadest perspective, erosion carves all of Zion into stairsteps of many levels.

The cliffs which border the Virgin River valley are uneven facades broken in many places by side canyons. These gorges are geologically new, not to be confused in age with the ancient rocks in which they are carved.

Icicle draperies, Weeping Rock. Freezing furthers erosion. Josef Muench photo.

Chasms and unexplored mesas. Eroded remnants of a once-continuous layer of stone.

An Ancient Lowland—Zion's layered rocks are not recent, not of our present era of upheaval and erosion, but of the past when the land was flat and near sea level. River plains, deltas, oceans and sandy deserts held sway for hundreds of millions of years. There was no hint that this part of the continent would some day rise high above the sea.

The lowland was an immense sinking basin. Its area fluctuated as borderlands rose and fell, and in the dimensions of time and geography, there were many irregularities. Gritty ruin washed down from distant highlands. Eon after eon, sand and mud were spread and respread by currents of air and water. Shelled animals and tiny plants that lived in the oceans also contributed; their calcium-rich remains became limestone. The crust of the earth continued to subside, and many kinds of sediment were preserved in layers.

There are clues to the past in the solidified sediments now uplifted and exposed. Geologists can tell much about ancient landscapes by studying these formations. Formations are the major groupings of sedimentary rock layers which are defined and named by geologists.

The Formations of Zion—Much of the Colorado Plateau was once part of the subsiding basinland. The formations of the Grand

Spring foliage adds gaiety to the canyon and beckons visitors out of their cars.

Red Arch Mountain, erosion in Gothic style. National Park Service photo.

Canyon and of Zion accumulated until they formed a great sunken "layer cake" nearly two miles deep. Present day landscapes reveal great uplift and erosion of those sediments.

The layered rocks which form the walls of Grand Canyon were laid down first. The higher layers, seen today at Zion Canyon, were deposited later. Grand Canyon-age rocks lie beneath Zion. Zion-age rocks once covered the Grand Canyon region, but they have been removed by erosion.

A few miles downstream from Zion Canyon, the total thickness of rock formations is nearly six thousand feet. This portion of the geological layer cake can be seen from the Big Plains road south of the park (photo, page 4). The massive block of the West Temple and Towers of the Virgin contains all six formations of Zion, from bottom to top: the Moenkopi, Chinle, Moenave, Kayenta, Navajo and Carmel (diagram, page 13). Most majestic is the Navajo Sandstone which towers as a two-thousand-foot cliff above the forested slopes of the Kayenta Formation.

Colorful formations below the Navajo disclose fascinating stories of the ancient basinland. However, we will concentrate on the environments of the Navajo and Kayenta, and leave descriptions of lower formations to other literature.

Gregory Butte from Hop Valley Trail. Morning shadows, emblazoned walls.

The Great Bend of Zion Canyon and Weeping Rock area from the top of Cable Mountain.

43

Two Environments in Flux—Where highlands rise today, the terrain of one hundred-eighty million years ago was low and flat. Silt and mud of the tropical Kayenta lowlands were spread layer on layer by sluggish streams. The Kayenta environment lasted for millions of years, but eventually it gave way to a different kind of deposition.

Sand-laden wind started blowing onto the Kayenta swamps and waterways, and gradually the Navajo desert smothered the verdant land. Over millions of years, the Kayenta was partly blotted out by dunes. At times the creeping sand won, only to lose briefly as the rivers surged back to reclaim the forward edge of the desert. There were many reversals, but finally the Kayenta rivers were choked completely by the shifting sand.

Parts of the vast Navajo desert may have been comparable to the Rub' al Khali of Saudi Arabia (photo, page 10) or to other Saharan-like terrain, where "*. . . vast accumulations of sand weighing millions of tons move inexorably, in regular fashion, over the surface of the country, growing, retaining their shape, even breeding, in a manner which, by its grotesque imitation of life, is vaguely disturbing to an imaginative mind,*" (Ref. 1).

The greatest enigma of the Navajo Formation is the origin of its quartz sand. Thousands of cubic miles of sand were deposited in an area which now covers parts of seven states. Probably, the dunes moved

South wall of Tucupit Point. Water seeps down behind wall slabs and honeycombs the cliffs.

44

south and east from distant eroding mountains long since vanished. No one knows for sure.

The Beauty of Crossbedding—The Navajo Sandstone erodes into wonderful patterns of wave-like lines—the "crossbedding" of ancient desert dunes (photos, pages 22 and 23). In the highlands of the park, the grain of the rock stirs our aesthetic senses. These gliding serpentine curves were formed in sand by wind and gravity. To the unartistic eye, the sweeping layers may be interesting studies in solid geometry. But to the imaginative mind, they conjure the form of ancient drifting sand—suggesting motion frozen in stone.

Artists know that a single graceful curve sets up a rhythmic motion of the eye, a pleasurable anticipation of visual return to previous positions. But in eroded crossbedding, countless sinuous lines stand out in near-parallel ranks.

Whereas the untrained eye sees curves in two dimensions, our knowing minds discern plates of stone extending into the rock. These are graceful curved slabs, once sheets of sand slipped from the crests of dunes. The study of ancient dunes is a whimsical pastime, for although the third dimension exists, it is seldom seen. Do the concealed structures sweep this way or that? The caprice of drifting sand is not predicted easily.

On some surfaces, each crossbed is scalloped repeatedly. Wavy shadows cast

The pitted, streaked face of the south wall of Tucupit Point from Double Arch alcove.

45

by the frilled edges transform ordinary stone into laceworks. Delicate lines make entrancing rhythms for the eye and play visual music in these sandstone symphonies. There is no end to beauty in the petrified desert of Zion.

The Sundance Sea—After millions of years, the Navajo desert was engulfed by sea water entering from the north. The Carmel Formation was deposited in the shallow embayment. These waters, which we call the Sundance Sea, were home to aqueous reptiles and innumerable shellfish.

In a few places near Zion that now are eight thousand feet above sea level, gargantuan oysters nearly a foot long are eroding from Carmel limestone. The evidence is that ancient sea bottoms rose to plateau heights, and that the mood in the earth's crust has changed since Sundance times. When did this change occur?

About seventy million years ago, restlessness stirred beneath the monotonous lowlands and inland seas of the Zion region. A new pattern of behavior gripped the land and started a geological revolution that has endured to the present. The ages marched forth in new cadence, carrying us to the present and portending the future.

Great Arch of Zion, an arched recess at the head of Pine Creek Canyon.

Gregory Butte and the free span of Kolob Arch from Death Point, mid-morning

46

Zion, A Restless Land...

As revolution began, widespread sinking ceased. For hundreds of millions of years, crustal unrest had disrupted distant lands. But then the upheavals came close to Zion. Beginning seventy million years ago, mountains rose along the length of North America, and part of Zion, on the eastern edge of one of the uplifts, was folded.

The Folded Mountains of Zion—In several places, the thick blanket of Grand Canyon and Zion-age strata were arched high above surrounding lands. As the earth's crust shortened in an east-west direction, the rocks buckled in the Kolob region, and the sixty-mile-long Kanarra Fold was formed. At Taylor Creek in Zion National Park, the strata were pushed so tightly that the west side of the Kanarra Fold turned over on top of its east side. Finally, stress could not be contained by mere bending, and the crumpled layers broke and faulted. Billions of tons of rock were shoved and shattered as the upper part of the fold slowly overrode the lower part along a great zone of slippage, the Taylor Creek Thrust Fault (Ref. 5).

On the Taylor Creek road, park visitors can visualize how compression deformed the rock. Upward warping of rock layers on the east side of the Kanarra Fold is seen in the gradual curved slant of the Finger

Joint-plane wall and red pond behind ancient landslide dam, South Canyon of Taylor Creek.

Canyon buttes (photo, page 12). Of course, these rocky points were not cut by erosion until relatively recent geologic times, but they do owe part of their bold prominence to the folding.

In most of Zion, the sedimentary layers were not disturbed, and they remained flat-lying. However, compression in the earth's crust did effect the rock layer cake in regions beyond Zion to the east where several isolated mountain ranges were up-folded.

In a broad sense, geological revolution had come to Zion. The vast lowlands had been broken by folding, and the region became less submissive to the slow, wide-spread sinking of earlier eras.

Erosion of the Folded Mountains—As deformation slackened, the rate of erosion exceeded the rate of mountain building, and the highlands were worn down. Gravel and sand washed into valleys and onto the remaining lowlands. Because clear paths to the ocean were blocked, fresh water lakes and streams occupied the low areas, and the basins filled with layers of ooze and rocky fragments. Again, Zion became a land of lakes and streams. It was an irregular basinland compared to the vast sinking areas that earlier had been filled with Grand Canyon and Zion layers, but nevertheless the regime of deposition had returned.

Nature is a master colorist. Vivid stripes on alcove walls, springline in the Kolob.

Today, the hardened ooze and the debris eroded from the folded mountains are seen in the colorful walls of Cedar Breaks and Bryce Canyon. The gritty rocks are called the "Pink Cliffs formation". They form the top sedimentary rock layers in southwestern Utah.

Grand Canyon, Zion and Cedar Breaks-age formations have been broadly compared to a three-layer cake. The analogy could be narrowed by saying that the baker was careless and distorted his cake before setting the pink layer on top. The Grand Canyon and Zion-age layers were broken by widespread folding before the Pink Cliffs layers were plastered unevenly across the top.

But the Pink Cliffs formation was not the final touch on the geological layer cake . . .

Fire Frosts the Cake—Like other cakes, the "plateau pastry" has frosting. On top of the Cedar Breaks layer is a glaze spread in part by hot gas. Even before the Pink Cliffs lakes had dried up, volcanic fires spewed out, heralding a new crescendo of the underground restlessness that started with the folding of the Grand Canyon and Zion-age layers.

Gas-rich magma rose from great depths and spilled onto the land. As molten rock frothed out, water in the magma, suddenly relieved of subterranean pressure, became explosive steam. This vapor shattered the foaming lava and carried white-hot splinters over hundreds of square miles. Burning clouds of ash swept along the ground at velocities of perhaps a hundred miles an hour. All animals in the way must have perished in a twinkling with little more to note their passing than astonished squeals and flashes of flame. The hard, glassy rock on Brian Head Mountain, near Cedar Breaks, was formed by fiery compaction of the shattered volcanic foam.

Glowing clouds were erupted often through long ages, but with passing time, the volcanoes changed in character.

Later eruptions of the Zion region were less violent than the incandescent holocausts that poured over the Cedar Breaks area some thirty million years ago. The recent eruptions left cinder cones such as Crater Hill and Firepit Knoll as well as the black lavas near Navajo Lake. This younger generation of volcanic rock contained less explosive vapor than the older lava, and it is different chemically too.

These changes in the lavas have accompanied the newer types of movement in the earth's crust. Rocks in the Zion area broke into great plateau blocks. And in geologically recent times, there is uplifting of the region which is only part of the prodigious rearing of the backbone of the Americas.

Creation of Plateaus—Why were the rocks of Zion elevated? The causes of uplift are not well known because our tools of scientific inquiry into the nature of the deep crust are very limited. We have only theories.

Although the causes of uplift are speculative, the surface effects are quite evident. In recent epochs, the Colorado Plateau has risen widely and gently, and most of its rock layers have remained horizontal. The Zion region has uplifted with little more disturbance than fracturing into large blocks along a few north-south faults. Zion Canyon is carved in the Markagunt Plateau block which is about thirty miles across and a hundred miles long (map, page 3). The Sevier Fault parallels the east side of the plateau, and the west side of the plateau is formed by the Hurricane Fault.

The Broken Land—Major faults, the large-scale result of earth stress, are difficult to see in entirety. But joints, the small fissures which break the rock in many places, are readily visible. These vertical fractures are caused by stress

Joint plane detail, patterns in Navajo Sandstone. Seven-hundred-foot-high portion of the south wall, Tucupit Point.

in the plateau blocks, and, unlike faults, little or no displacement occurs along them.

Joints in great number pervade this land. They cleave the walls of Zion and become zones of rapid erosion (photo, page 26). Without them, the canyons would not erode with such strong vertical character. While layered rocks give shape to tablelands and lead our eyes over lines in repose, joints give rise to spires that exalt our senses and draw our vision skyward.

Engrossing patterns can be seen on joint surfaces, particularly where rock on one side of the fracture has toppled away and exposed the opposite plane to view (photo, page 51). If you follow the sheer walls in joint canyons, you will find unexpected beauty. On these immense stone murals are bold fluted patterns and delicate shell-like etchings. Neither erosion nor the wind of ancient dunes carved these reliefs—they are the result of earth stress.

Pathways for Erosion—Joints, the pathways for erosion, are most noticeable in Navajo Sandstone. Runoff from rain and snow follows the fissures, dissolves the mineral cements in stone, and weakens the land internally. The ability of joints to channel water is seen in angular drainage patterns. As water follows the crisscrossing fractures, Zion is carved into blocks surrounded by narrow canyons (photo, page 39). The

Slickrock terrain eroded in upper Navajo Sandstone. White Arch in the distance.

Potholes and pools. Flowing sculptures in stone carved by water during floods.

Great White Throne and other singular monoliths are unfractured blocks isolated by deep erosion.

It is the bold verticality of joints in Navajo Sandstone that combines with the horizontality of lower formations to give Zion its erosional framework (photo, page 27). Nature's architecture at Zion is formed not by construction but by disassembly.

Erosion Destroys the Land...

A movie made of Zion for the last million years at a rate of one picture frame per hundred years would run eight minutes. It would be the story of recent geological times, but what an incredible spectacle it would be. We would see immediately that stability here is illusory, and that Zion seems to stand still only because we are short-lived.

Storms through time are ushering the lands to the sea. Like fungus in a rotting stump, the branching system of streams and joints interweaves the land and subdivides intricately to gain destructive purchase on the plateaus. Zion decomposes externally and within, wherever water circulates on the surface or along fissures.

Kolob Arch in Zion's wilderness. Vertical wedge of red sandstone, partly collapsed.

White Arch, red tapestries. Weathered iron streaks the walls and stains the land.

Zion's most recent rock cycle, the subject of this story, has three parts: deposition uplift and erosion. We are living in the time of the last two parts and are trying to find the meaning of this erosional destruction

The Carving of Zion Canyon—The chapters of uplift and erosion began about ten million years ago when the terrain was low not far above sea level. The ancestral Virgin River meandered on subdued topography. As the Markagunt block slowly rose, the river became erosive and began denuding the land of its layered rocks. The strata were stripped back, each layer receding according to its own character and its relationship to other layers.

With sediment borne by water, the Virgin scoured through the Navajo Sandstone. And under the effect of gravity, fragments of formations beneath the Navajo tumbled slowly toward the voracious river. The result is Zion Canyon.

The lower, wide part of the canyon is a stair-stepped land with many colorful rock layers exposed in benches and cliffs.

But upper Zion Canyon narrows between sheer walls of Navajo Sandstone, and there the Virgin River changes greatly in its style of excavation.

The Narrows—Many landscape features at Zion owe their existence to the upward change from shale to sandstone at the

"Hoodoo" and white-washed wall, Johnson Canyon. Grotesque or beautiful?

boundary between the Kayenta and Navajo formations. Where the river crosses this plane in Zion Canyon, the Narrows begin and continue upstream. Downstream from the Narrows, the river valley is widened as soft red sediments of the Kayenta fall and are washed toward the river. But in the Narrows, where the Virgin River is in Navajo Sandstone alone, the stream cuts downward in sheer slots of its own making.

Most visitors cannot see the real Narrows because there is no practical way to build a road or even a trail into a chasm often filled wall to wall by the river. Back country enthusiasts wade and swim through the whole dark labyrinth from the top of the Markagunt Plateau to the Temple of Sinawava. It is a thirteen mile trek. The experience is unique; no other canyon in the world has such narrowness as compared to depth. Near Deep Creek, the Narrows is over a thousand feet deep and less than twenty feet wide at the bottom (photo, page 68).

Man wades into the gorge timidly and looks for his bearings, for any indications of downward progress. As the slot deepens, the traveler loses contact with the outside world. He resigns his drenched, wearisome sloggings into the darkening void ahead. Overhead, the walls warp in and out, often locking out the narrow blue strip of sky. In some places, sunrise comes a few minutes before noon, and sunset follows within an hour.

Sandstone pillar near East Entrance is shielded by a hard, iron-rich cap.

57

Sunlight enters in yellowish shafts and is cast into the swift green water. This chasm is like an immense cathedral, but the nave is narrower and ten times higher than in any church built by man. It is a temple to erosion in rock made of ancient desert sand.

Streams issue noisily into the main chasm through fissures narrower than a forearm, and in the deep gurgles there is entrancing music. But apprehension spoils the effect. The waders glance up and see enormous logs jammed sideways from wall to wall twenty feet above the stream. Matted flotsam is plastered high against the walls.

These masses of debris are forceful reminders that the Narrows is a waterspout for storms, a treacherous funnel in which human life has been lost. Flash floods surge through in thirty-foot crests, and in many stretches there is no place for hapless adventurers to climb to safety.

Sandstone Corridors—Sometimes, hikers in the Narrows hear the

Zion Canyon from end of the East Rim Trail. Navajo Sandstone forms most of the walls in the upper canyon.

The scenic threshold. Mouth of Zion Canyon from the Big Plains road.

stony thumps of cobbles colliding in hollows or "potholes" on the channel floor. The stones are driven by swirling backwashes of the stream. In floods, these hard rock balls rapidly abrade their sandstone pits. The tubelike chambers of Zion's narrow gorges are bored by pommeling stones in fluid motion.

Uncanny feelings affect the person who walks the twisted corridor between towering walls of a pothole trench. It is like treading between ranks of gigantic knees. The route twists downward into darker sandstone dungeons, and on each turn, the wary explorer half expects to confront a gnome.

Between the looming walls there is little to set the imagination at ease. However, when viewed in sunlight, the convolutions are so graceful that they vie with crossbedding in beauty of form. A few lines of deep potholes have been breached by erosion and are open to view (photo, page 64). Here are undulating planes in rhythmic balance (photo, page 53). It is hard to believe that churning water could produce such masterpieces.

Where the curved surfaces are in Navajo Sandstone, we delight in seeing them in combination with lines of crossbedding. Carved in former dunes are flowing planes showing freedom of ancient wind and recent water.

Partly collapsed wall slab, an arch of simple form and pleasing texture.

The Virgin River on a pleasant summer day, lower Zion Canyon.

Although these sculpturings are doomed to removal by erosion, much potential for beauty lies in rock yet to be exposed. As running water melts this rugged land, there is continual creation of pleasing form.

Erosion of the Lower Navajo Sandstone—Nature is not haphazard in removing the ancient desert sand from Zion. She breaks the Navajo layer in a systematic manner that is easily understood in what we observe in the rocks.

The most important division between two formations at Zion is the contact between the Kayenta and Navajo. Without the Navajo Sandstone, there would be no Zion. However, without the Kayenta shales beneath the sandstone, the face of Zion would be entirely different.

The Navajo layer, composed of tiny rounded quartz grains, is porous throughout and saturated with water in its lower part. Water percolates between the sand grains, seeps down joints, and issues in springs at the base of the formation where clay in the underlying Kayenta hinders further downward flow. Weeping Rock, the Hanging Gardens and countless seeps lie at the base of the Navajo Sandstone on the master springline of Zion (photo, page 38).

Along the lower Navajo cliffs, spring water dissolves cements in the sandstone, and the rock is gradually weakened and undermined. No wonder rockfalls are so common to the lower part of the formation (photo, page 18). At Zion, there are two noticeable patterns followed by erosion in the lower Navajo Sandstone: development of

Single raindrop. The impact of falling rain contributes to erosion. U. S. Naval Research Laboratory photo.

Trillionfold raindrops, flood in late summer. The river roars seaward with spoils of erosional battle.

canyon walls at an angle to and parallel to joints.

In the first case, erosion cuts across the joints, and the resulting cliffs break away in vertical columns (photo, page 7). An example is the stately north face of the Watchman, which is rifted by joints (photo, page 27). From these walls, huge pilasters of sandstone topple down as their under-footings are weakened.

In the second case, walls are formed parallel to the joints, and the slabs fall away slowly in a way that has been com-pared to removing slice after slice from an enormous loaf of bread. This pattern of erosion is exemplified by the smooth north wall of Lady Mountain. Usually, the rock does not weaken uniformly, and the slabs collapse bit by bit. Many beautiful stone faces have been formed by gradual break-ing of joint slabs (photo, page 60).

Water often trickles down joints behind walls and dissolves the carbonate cement in the rock. A slab may become honey-combed like wormwood and finally cannot support its own weight (photo, page 44). In what shape does failure occur? Some-times in a graceful arch, the path of least resistance to the pull of gravity (photo, page 55). If the slab is weakened on lines of crossbedding, or if it is crossed by joints, an arch of ideal shape may not result. Then the fracture has an irregular outline

Breached potholes and amber pool. The elegance of simple forms and subtle colors.

Water-worn crossbedding. Harmonious intersection of lines and planes.

(photo, page 41). Many of Zion's arches and vaulted panels depart from the theoretical curve. In nature, the ideal is seldom realized, and the perfect is rarely seen.

Erosion of the Upper Navajo Sandstone— The lower Navajo Sandstone collapses along joints and forms sheer walls and crags. However, land forms in the upper part of the formation are rounded, possibly because the terrain on top was eroded for a long time during the early history of the canyon. Also, the upper white sandstone has less of the red iron oxide cement that binds the lower Navajo so well. Erosion of the upper Navajo Sandstone is largely by crumbling and peeling of the rounded surfaces.

The upper Navajo terrain, particularly in the Kolob area, is described well by Clarence Dutton: "... *It is a veritable wonderland. If we descend to it we shall perceive numberless rock forms of nameless shapes, but often grotesque and ludicrous, starting up from the earth as isolated freaks or standing in clusters and rows along the white walls of sandstone. They bear little likeness to anything we can think of, and yet they tease the imagination to find something whereunto they may be likened. Yet the forms are in a certain sense very definite and many of them look merry and farcical. The land here is full of comedy. It is a singular display of Nature's*

Kolob Terrace country and the dissected tablelands of Zion from Deertrap Mountain.

Double Arch alcove, an undermined spring-line. Vaulted ceiling and seepage streaks.

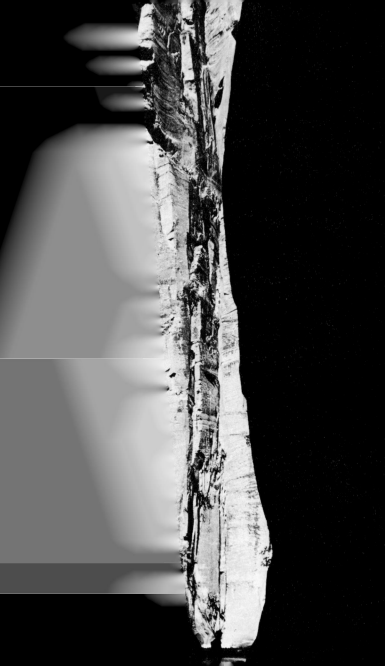

art mingled with nonsense. It is well named the Colob, for the word has no ascertainable meaning, and yet it sounds as if it ought to have one . . ." (Ref.3).

In sculpturing stone, nature may overstep our sense of beauty and stumble into absurdity. All sorts of whale-backs and baldheads, domes and beehives, and knobs and hobgoblins decorate the slickrock areas of upper Navajo (photo, page 57). The delicate lines in ancient sand dunes crisscross the rock and, in many places, this cross-bedding is broken by cracks that produce odd biscuitworks and checkerboards (photo, page 34).

History of the Canyon—Visitors often ask why the lower Navajo is deep red and the upper part is glistening white. The division between the two colors is an undulating line halfway up the canyon walls. This color boundary and other land forms can be explained by the stages of down-cutting of Zion Canyon by the Virgin River.

In a few places, there are three discontinuous terraces on the sides of lower Zion Canyon; they are remnants of valley floors cut long ago by the Virgin River. These fea-tures suggest that the Markagunt Plateau was uplifted in at least three distinct pulses, and that the river reacted vigorously each time with renewed downcutting, followed by gradual widening and the establishment of a new valley floor at a level lower than the preceding one. The red-white color boundary in the Navajo probably marks the ground water level beneath one of these old valleys. The red iron minerals may have been dissolved in the upper part of the formation and carried down to the

Hiker in Narrows where the gorge is fifty times deeper than wide. Roland Wauer photo.

water table which, at that time, stood at the top of the lower red part of the Navajo Sandstone. Apparently, there was no such water level of long duration in the Kolob because, there, the Navajo Sandstone is red throughout (photo, page 42).

Glaciers had no part in shaping Zion Canyon, but the Virgin may have been a larger river during the four times that moist climate came to the Southwest during the glacial epoch. Increased runoff may have been related to the stages of downcutting in the canyon.

Earthquakes on faults of the Markagunt Plateau speak for the continuing restlessness of Zion. Uplift and downcutting may be as rapid now as at any time in the past. Although enormous amounts of rock have wasted from the plateaus and washed to the sea, much erosion lies ahead in the future.

Seen from the canyon rim at midday, the Virgin River shimmers like a silver ribbon. Who would guess that such a lovely spangle is a destructive link between past and present? It works toward realization of Universal order. Nature's forces are far from spent, and Zion moves toward fulfillment of a natural cycle.

Sky reflections and sunlight in a pothole pool make confusing but interesting patterns.

Fulfillment of a Cycle...

New life arises from the materials of old and takes its sustenance from sunlight, moisture and air. Rock, on the other hand, is doomed when exposed to the atmosphere. It decomposes and disintegrates, loses its identity, and passes on, often to be formed anew.

When sediment is finally deposited, trapped in layers in low, stable places, it may become new rock. Continuance of its new identity depends on quiet burial and lack of change. But change is inevitable, and disturbance by earth forces seems certain.

Zion, a land in upheaval, is more than a static interface between earth and sky. It is transfigured by erosion into ever-changing surfaces that dissolve the order of ancient rock into apparent disorder. Matter must gather in more stable places than high plateaus, so it is called downward by gravity to satisfy nature's demands for equilibrium. This is a natural scheme that lessens chaos through the rearrangement of earth material. Erosion breaks down the highs and fills in the lows—it tends to equalize landscapes and ultimately to re-

Hiker on upper precipitous section of the West Rim Trail. Crossbedded Navajo Sandstone.

Colorado River Delta. The burial of plateaus, fulfillment of a cycle. John Shelton photo.

70

duce even continents to sea level. But our convulsive globe keeps rejuvenating the lands, and erosion never seems to achieve its final goal.

Through uplift, sediments eroded from former lands may be exposed again. On this restless planet, the biographies of sand grains are medleys of random journeys.

Departure of the Broken Land—In late summer, dynamic skies steal the show from the land. Like warships, clouds rise with sails billowing full and white. Their underdecks are daubed with black, sign of impending battle against earth. Thundering flotillas advance on sandstone bulwarks and gray rain shadows spill down. Water free and wild begins its surge to the sea.

The usual placid green innocence of the Virgin is misleading, and to many people it is nothing more than a pleasant creek for wading. But after thundershowers, the Virgin swells to flood (photo, page 63). It seethes like a thing alive, a serpent devouring red watery tons of mud and sand from countless tributaries. We stand awestruck as enormous boulders crash and split asunder. Uprooted cottonwoods tumble and upend like jackstraws. And the torrent roars seaward with spoils of erosional battle.

The mass boils down channel to join the mightier brother of the Virgin, the Colorado River. Finally, mingled with debris

Disintegration of rock, the face of Zion.
Red iron oxide weathers from a land in ruin.

72